# I·N·S·I·D·E

# ITALY

Ian James

Photography: Chris Fairclough

**Franklin Watts**

London · New York · Sydney · Toronto

# CONTENTS

1988 Franklin Watts
12a Golden Square
London W1

Published in the USA by
Franklin Watts Inc.
387 Park Avenue South
New York, N.Y. 10016

Franklin Watts Australia
14 Mars Road
Lane Cove
NSW 2066

Design: Edward Kinsey
Illustrations: Hayward Art Group

UK ISBN: 0 86313 711 3
US ISBN: 0-531-10613-6
Library of Congress Catalog
Card Number: 88-50193

Phototypeset by Lineage, Watford
Printed in Belgium

Additional Photographs:
Allsport 19, Zoe Dominic 22 (T);
Italian State Tourist Office 5 (T), 21, 22;
Mansell Collection 8; Popperfoto 9

Front cover: Chris Fairclough
Back cover: Chris Fairclough

# The land

Italy is a large country in southern Europe. It consists mainly of a peninsula, a long land mass shaped like a boot, which is surrounded by arms of the Mediterranean Sea. Italy also includes two large, mainly mountainous islands – Sicily and Sardinia – and several small ones.

Mountains and hills cover four-fifths of Italy. The highest mountains are the Alps in the north. The tallest peak is Mont Blanc, which rises 4,807 m (15,771 ft) on Italy's border with France. The Alps contain many beautiful lakes.

Many rivers flow from the Alps into Italy's largest lowland, the mainly flat Po Valley. The Po, which is 670 km (416 miles) long, is Italy's longest river. It flows across northern Italy into the Adriatic Sea.

Below: **Italy's Mediterranean Coast has many attractive beaches and resorts.**

Above: **Mount Vesuvius, a volcano in southern Italy, overlooks Naples.**

Left: **The Dolomites in northeastern Italy are part of the Alps.**

South of the Po valley are the Apennine mountains. This range forms the backbone of the Italian peninsula. It contains some flat basins, but it is mainly rugged country.

Above: **Lake d'Orta is one of several beautiful lakes in northern Italy.**

A chain of volcanoes runs though southern Italy. It includes Vesuvius near Naples, the small, volcanic Lipari Islands and Mount Etna in Sicily. Vesuvius erupted with great force in AD79 and destroyed two towns, Herculaneum and Pompeil. Vesuvius last erupted in 1944. Etna erupts more frequently than Vesuvius.

The mountains of northern Italy have cold, snowy winters and sunny summers, and plenty of rain throughout the year. In the south, summers are dry and hot, with occasional thunderstorms. Winters are mild and moist.

# The people and their history

Throughout history, many people, including Greeks, Phoenicians, Gauls and Normans, have settled in Italy. One early group, the Etruscans, who probably came from the east, founded a civilization in central Italy.

Etruscan kings once ruled Rome. But the Romans overthrew the Etruscans in 509BC and made Rome a republic. The Romans conquered a large empire, including about a quarter of Europe and parts of North Africa and the Middle East. They brought law and order to the conquered peoples. Ruins of great Roman cities, temples, roads and bridges can be seen throughout Italy.

The Roman Empire finally ended in AD476, when Germanic tribes defeated the last Roman emperor, Romulus Augustulus.

Below: **The ancient ruins of the Forum in Rome that was the heart of government during the Roman Empire.**

For most of the time after the fall of the Roman Empire, Italy was divided into small states or it was ruled by foreign powers. Some city-states, such as Florence and Venice, achieved great wealth. In the 14th and 15th centuries, they helped artists who led a great artistic movement called the Renaissance.

Spain, Austria and France all ruled Italy for periods between the 16th and 19th centuries. Most of Italy was united in 1861, largely through the efforts of a patriot, Giuseppe Garibaldi. It became a kingdom under Victor Emmanuel II, former King of Sardinia.

Italy entered World War I in 1915 on the side of the Allies. It gained some land, including the city of Trieste. But the war proved very costly and Italy faced many economic problems in the 1920s.

Below: **The Italian patriot Giuseppe Garibaldi helped Victor Emmanuel (on the white horse) to become King of Italy.**

Right: **The map shows major cities, ports and routes in Italy.**

Trieste

Milan

Venice

Verona

Turin

Genoa

Bologna

Leghorn

Florence

Major cities

Main ports

Main routeways

Rome

Naples

Bari

Brindisi

Taranto

Messina

Palermo

Catania

Augusta

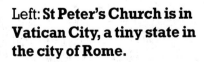

Left: **St Peter's Church is in Vatican City, a tiny state in the city of Rome.**

Rome became capital of Italy in 1870. But this beautiful city, which stands on the Tiber River about 25 km (16 miles) from the sea, is often called the Eternal City, because it has been a heart of civilization for more than 2,000 years. Central Rome contains impressive ruins, including the Forum, from which the Roman Empire was ruled, and the huge Colosseum.

Rome has many fine churches. The best known is St. Peter's in Vatican City. Vatican City, the headquarters of the Roman Catholic Church, is the World's smallest independent nation. It covers an area of only 44 hectares (108.7 acres) in northwestern Rome.

Most people in Rome have jobs in commerce, government and other services. Only one in five works in industries.

Below: **The plan of Rome shows some of its famous buildings, streets and squares.**

1 **St.Peter's Church**
2 **Castel Sant' Angelo (a Medieval fortress)**
3 **Piazza Navona**
4 **Palazzo Farnese**
5 **The Pantheon**
6 **Piazza di Spagna and Spanish Steps**
7 **Via Vittorio Veneto**
8 **Ancient Roman ruins**
9 **The Colosseum**

Above: **Meals are important family occasions.**

Left: **Mixed pasta dishes are often served as the first course of a meal.**

# Food

Each region of Italy has its own special dishes. For example, pizza, which is now popular throughout the world, originally came from Naples. Bologna is known for its sausages, Parma for its smoked ham and Milan for the thick soup, minestrone. Italy is famous for its pasta, including lasagne, macaroni, spaghetti and vermicelli. Pasta, which is made from flour, is often eaten as a first course, followed by a meat dish or salad, and a dessert or fruit.

Breakfast for most people consists of a roll and coffee. Lunch is usually the main meal, while dinner is a lighter meal. Many Italians drink wine with their lunch and dinner, though mineral water is also popular. Famous Italian wines include Chianti, Frascati, Marsala, Soave and Valpolicella.

Below: **Many people shop in open-air markets or small shops.**

# Family life

Two-thirds of Italian families own their homes. Many city people live in apartments. But there are plenty of modern houses with gardens in the suburbs. In recent years, living standards have risen. By 1988, 76 out of every 100 Italian households owned a car. Home furnishings have improved greatly and four out of every five households have a washing machine.

Families in rural areas are generally less prosperous. The average income in Italy south of Rome is less than three-fifths of that in central and northern Italy. Unemployment is also twice as high in the south.

Family life is valued highly by most Italians, who keep in close contact with their relatives. Many families enjoy entertaining their relatives and friends at home.

Left: **A family outside their apartment block in Turin.**

Left: **Most Italian apartments have balconies where people can dry their laundry.**

Below: **An Italian family in the living room.**

# The arts

Italy is known for its superb works of art. Some of the world's finest artists, including Leonardo da Vinci (1452-1519), who painted the famous *Mona Lisa*, and Michelangelo (1475-1564), another painter and sculptor of a huge statue of David, were Italians. Leading Italian writers include Dante Alighieri (1265-1321), author of *The Divine Comedy*, and Giovanni Boccaccio (1313-1375), author of *The Decameron*.

Italy is probably even better known as the home of opera, which began in the early 17th century. Such Italian operas as *La Traviata* by Giuseppe Verdi (1813-1901) and *La Bohème* by Giacomo Puccini (1858-1924) are played regularly throughout the world. Italy has produced many great singers.

Below: **Florence is a city of magnificent buildings, churches and museums housing art treasures.**

21

Above: **A scene from the opera *Aida*, by Verdi, being performed in Verona.**

Left: **The ceiling of the Sistine Chapel in the Vatican was painted by Michelangelo.**

# Farming

Farming employs 12 out of every 100 workers in Italy. The main farm region is the Po valley, where wheat, maize and rice are grown. Mulberry leaves are grown to feed silkworms. Cattle are reared in the Po Valley and also on farms in the Alps, which make dairy products. Vines grow on flat terraces on the lower slopes. Italy makes about a fifth of the world's wine.

Grapes are also grown in central and southern Italy. Here the soil is generally poorer than in the north, except for some fertile basins in the Apennine Mountains and near volcanoes, such as in the Bay of Naples.

Almonds, citrus fruits (such as oranges), olives and wheat, are other major crops. Sheep are common. Their milk is used to make cheese.

Below: **Olive groves in Tuscany. Italy is the world's largest producer of olives after Greece.**

Above: **A farmer at work in the Po Valley. In the background are grape vines.**

Below: **Italy produces a huge variety of fruits and vegetables both for the home market and export.**

# Industry

Italy produces some oil and natural gas. But it has to import both of these fuels and coal to meet its needs. The country has resources of water power. In the 1980s hydroelectric power stations supplied nearly a quarter of Italy's total electricity supply.

Many minerals are mined, but in small quantities. Only mercury and sulphur are produced in sufficient quantities to meet the country's needs. The rest must be imported. Because many materials are imported, many of Italy's factories are found in sea ports, such as Genoa. The country's main industrial region is in the triangle formed by Genoa, Turin and Milan. Industry employs 41 per cent of Italy's workers and manufacturing is Italy's most valuable activity.

Below: **Italy is one of the world's leading producers of cars. They are noted for design.**

| | |
|---|---|
|  | Industry |
| | Petroleum |
| | Cattle |
| | Sheep |
| | Wheat |
| | Rice |
| | Grapes |
| | Olives |
| | Fishing |
| | Mulberry Leaves (for silk) |
| | Citrus fruits |

**Right: The map shows some of the economic activities in Italy.**

Textiles, clothing, leather and footwear are major industrial products. Many items are superbly designed and they are exported. Florence, Milan and Rome are the main cities for the clothing and fashion industry. One famous fashion house, Benneton, is known for its knitwear, which is not too expensive.

Elegant design is important in the success of other industries, including the production of elegant cars. Fiat is Italy's largest privately owned company. It produces not only Fiat cars, but it also owns Alfa Romeo, Autobianchi, Ferrari and Lancia. Italy has many food-processing industries, huge chemical plants and large steel mills. Today, Italy is the world's sixth leading producer of steel and one of the world's top ten industrial countries.

Below: **Italian clothes have a worldwide reputation for quality and design.**

# Looking to the future

Italy was a founder member of the European Economic Community, which was established in 1957. It was the poorest of the first six members. But today it is one of the four richest nations in the 12-nation Community, along with West Germany, France and Britain.

Only a few years ago, Italy was called the "sick man of the European Community." It suffered from political instability and terrorism throughout most of the 1960s and 1970s. In the 1980s, however it made great strides. By the late 1980s, its industries were booming and political instability seemed to be a thing of the past. As a result, the tourist industry was continuing to grow and living standards for most people were rising sharply.

Below: **A school in Turin. Italians can now look forward to a bright future.**

Despite its successes, Italy still faces many problems. Poverty still exists, especially in the south. The development of industry has also led to pollution, especially around the cities and factory areas.

Italy is also facing similar problems to other western industrial countries. For example, its population is ageing and drug addiction is becoming more common. Italy also has a large "black economy." This means that large numbers of people get income from jobs (often second jobs) on which they do not pay taxes. However, some people think that the large "black economy" is a good sign, showing that the people are enterprising. Another important sign for the future is the growth of new high-technology industries.

Above: **Italy has many high-technology industries.**

29

# Facts about Italy

**Area:**
301,225 sq km
(116,304 sq miles)

**Population:**
57,350,850 (1987 est)

**Capital:**
Rome

**Largest cities:**
Rome (pop 2,826,000)
Milan (1,515,000)
Naples (1,206,000)
Turin (1,035,000)
Genoa (736,000)
Palermo (720,000)

**Official language:**
Italian

**Religion:**
Christianity

**Main exports:**
Textiles, chemicals,
footwear, iron and steel,
machinery, vehicles

**Unit of currency:**
Lira

## Italy compared with other countries.

**Italy** 187 per sq. km.

**Britain** 232 per sq. km.

**USA** 26 per sq. km.

**Australia** 2 per sq. km.

Above: **How many people?
Italy is heavily populated
compared with some other
countries.**

Below: **How large? Italy has
a small land area compared
with some countries.**

USA          Australia          Italy   UK

Below: **Italian money and
stamps.**

# Index

PRINTED IN BELGIUM BY

proost
INTERNATIONAL BOOK PRODUCTION